For my parents,
who gave me the love of nature and art

With love,
Anne

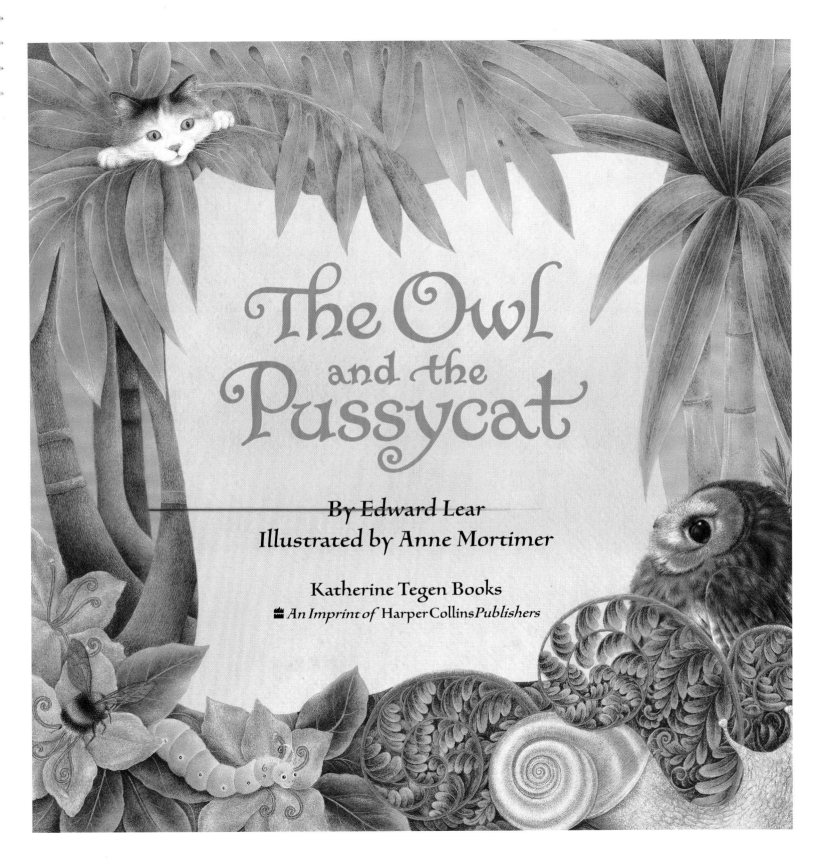

The Owl and the Pussycat

By Edward Lear

Illustrated by Anne Mortimer

Katherine Tegen Books
An Imprint of HarperCollins*Publishers*

The owl and the pussycat
went to sea
In a beautiful pea-green boat.

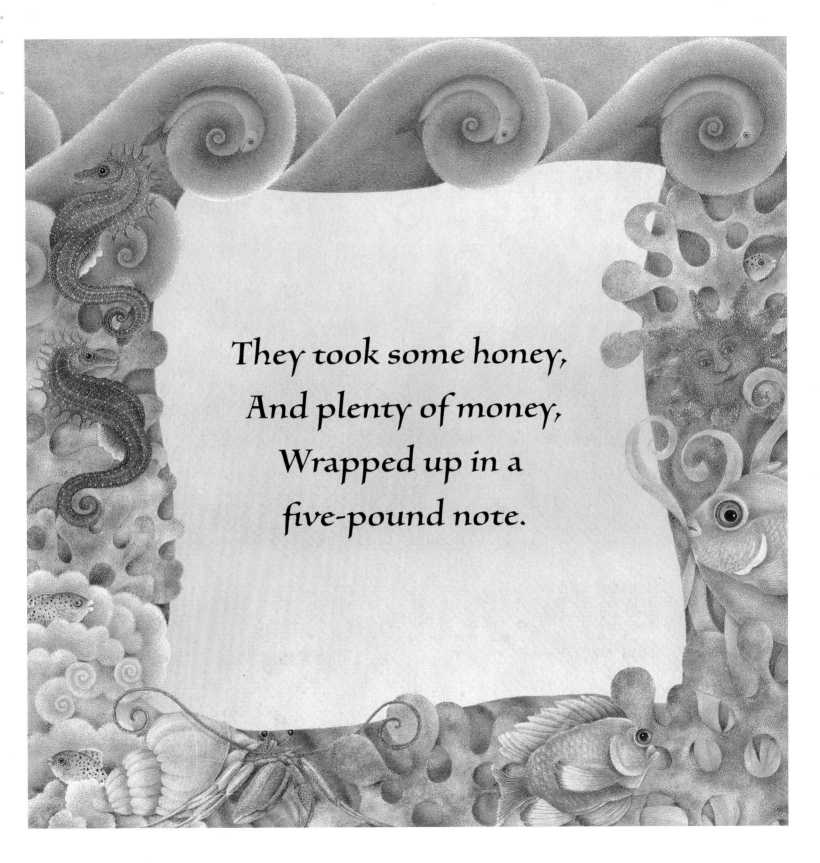

They took some honey,
And plenty of money,
Wrapped up in a
five-pound note.

The Owl looked up to the stars above,

And sang to a small guitar,

"O lovely Pussy! O Pussy, my love,

What a beautiful Pussy you are,

You are,

You are!

What a beautiful Pussy you are!"

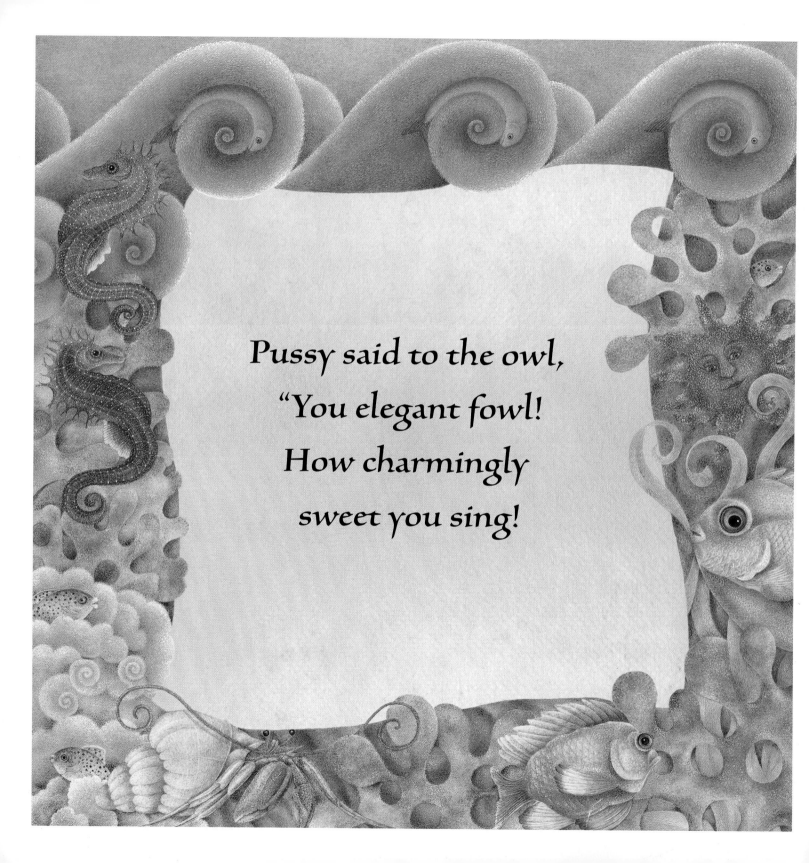

Pussy said to the owl,
"You elegant fowl!
How charmingly
sweet you sing!

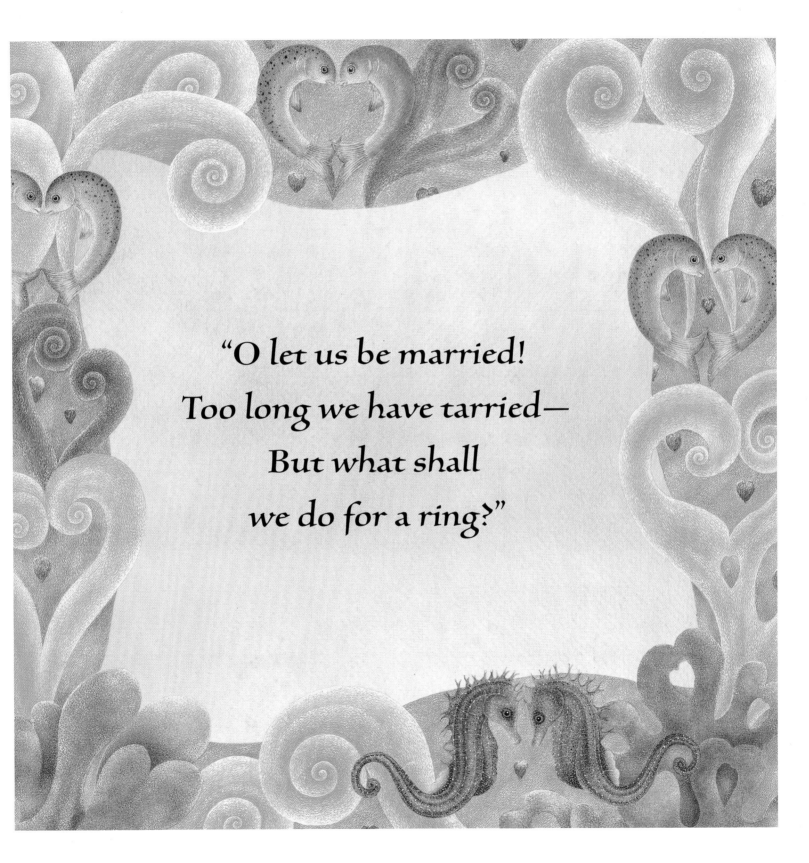

"O let us be married!
Too long we have tarried—
But what shall
we do for a ring?"

They sailed away,
For a year and a day,
To the land where
the bong tree grows.

And there in the wood
a Piggywig stood
With a ring at the
end of his nose,

His nose,

His nose.

With a ring at the
end of his nose.

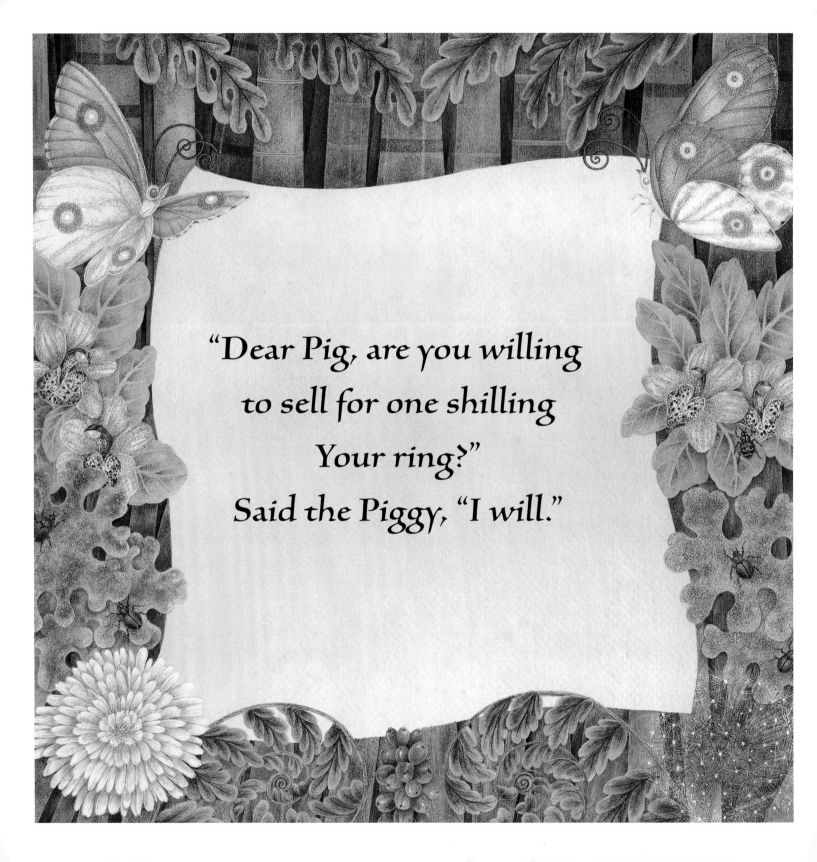

"Dear Pig, are you willing
to sell for one shilling
Your ring?"
Said the Piggy, "I will."

So they took it away and
were married next day
By the Turkey who
lives on the hill.

They dined on mince,
and slices of quince,
Which they ate with a runcible spoon.

And hand in hand,
on the edge of the sand,
They danced by the
light of the moon,
The moon,
The moon.
They danced by the
light of the moon.

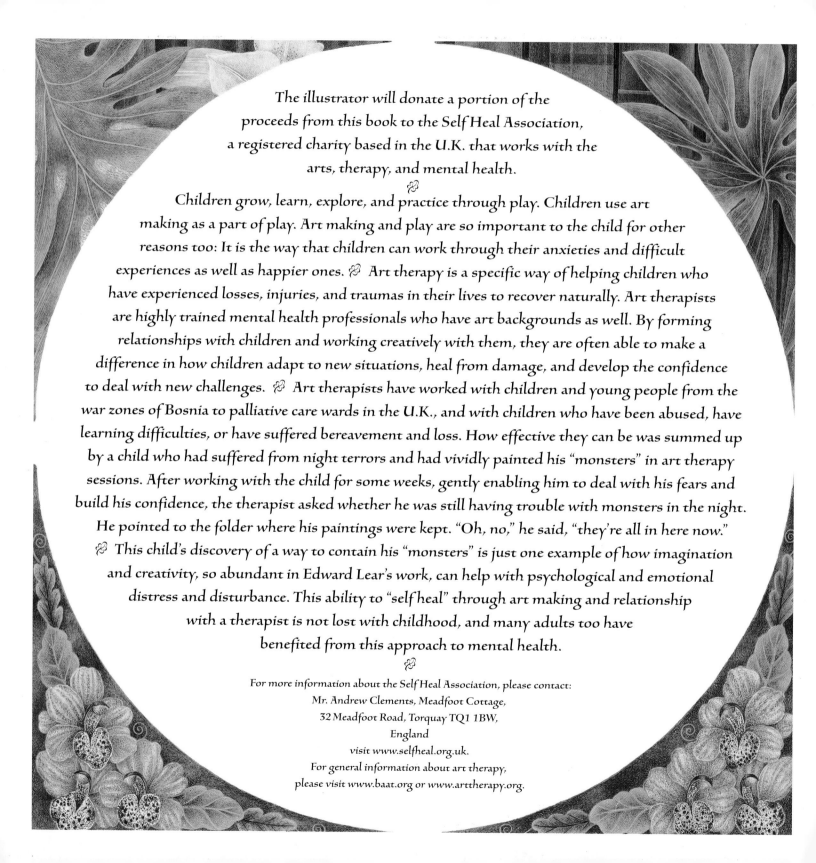

The illustrator will donate a portion of the
proceeds from this book to the Self Heal Association,
a registered charity based in the U.K. that works with the
arts, therapy, and mental health.

Children grow, learn, explore, and practice through play. Children use art
making as a part of play. Art making and play are so important to the child for other
reasons too: It is the way that children can work through their anxieties and difficult
experiences as well as happier ones. Art therapy is a specific way of helping children who
have experienced losses, injuries, and traumas in their lives to recover naturally. Art therapists
are highly trained mental health professionals who have art backgrounds as well. By forming
relationships with children and working creatively with them, they are often able to make a
difference in how children adapt to new situations, heal from damage, and develop the confidence
to deal with new challenges. Art therapists have worked with children and young people from the
war zones of Bosnia to palliative care wards in the U.K., and with children who have been abused, have
learning difficulties, or have suffered bereavement and loss. How effective they can be was summed up
by a child who had suffered from night terrors and had vividly painted his "monsters" in art therapy
sessions. After working with the child for some weeks, gently enabling him to deal with his fears and
build his confidence, the therapist asked whether he was still having trouble with monsters in the night.
He pointed to the folder where his paintings were kept. "Oh, no," he said, "they're all in here now."
This child's discovery of a way to contain his "monsters" is just one example of how imagination
and creativity, so abundant in Edward Lear's work, can help with psychological and emotional
distress and disturbance. This ability to "self heal" through art making and relationship
with a therapist is not lost with childhood, and many adults too have
benefited from this approach to mental health.

For more information about the Self Heal Association, please contact:
Mr. Andrew Clements, Meadfoot Cottage,
32 Meadfoot Road, Torquay TQ1 1BW,
England
visit www.selfheal.org.uk.
For general information about art therapy,
please visit www.baat.org or www.arttherapy.org.

Edward Lear

was an accomplished nineteenth-century artist, illustrator, and
writer known for his nonsensical poetry, including limericks. Born
in England in 1812, he was the second youngest of twenty-one children.
Before he was an author of silly books, he worked extensively as an illustrator
for scientific books on birds, and he also worked as a landscape painter. In 1846
he published his first book of nonsense verse and pictures, A Book of Nonsense.
The book was so popular that he published a number of others as well, his most
famous piece being "The Owl and the Pussycat." Lear had a flair for writing and
especially loved to make up words, such as "runcible spoon." He wrote an
incomplete sequel to "The Owl and the Pussycat" that begins:

Our mother was the Pussycat,
Our father was the Owl,
So we are partly little beasts
And partly little fowl. . . .

The Owl and the Pussycat
Illustrations copyright © 2006 by Anne Mortimer
Manufactured in China. All rights reserved. No part of this book may be used or reproduced in any manner whatsoever
without written permission except in the case of brief quotations embodied in critical articles and reviews.
For information address HarperCollins Children's Books,
a division of HarperCollins Publishers, 1350 Avenue of the Americas, New York, NY 10019.
www.harperchildrens.com
Library of Congress Cataloging-in-Publication Data
Lear, Edward, 1812–1888.
The owl and the pussycat / by Edward Lear ; illustrated by Anne Mortimer. — 1st edition.
p. cm. — Summary: After a courtship voyage of a year and a day, Owl and Pussy
finally buy a ring from Piggy and are blissfully married. ISBN-10: 0-06-027228-7 — ISBN-10: 0-06-027229-5 (lib. bdg.)
ISBN-13: 978-0-06-027228-9 — ISBN-13: 978-0-06-027229-6 (lib. bdg.)
1. Animals—Juvenile poetry. 2. Children's poetry, English. [1. Nonsense verses. 2. Animals—Poetry. 3. English poetry.]
I. Title. II. Mortimer, Anne, ill. PR4879.L2 O9 2006 [821'.8]—dc22 2003015476 CIP AC
Typography by Elynn Cohen 1 2 3 4 5 6 7 8 9 10 ❖ First Edition